Never Summer

Poems From Thin Air

CHRIS RANSICK

Never Summer

Poems From Thin Air

Chris Ransick

CONUN
DRUM
PRESS

AN IMPRINT OF BOWER HOUSE

DENVER

Library of Congress Cataloging-in-Publication Data
ISBN: 978-1-938633-23-2

Some of these poems have been published in *Appalachia, Bakunin, Black River Review, Calliope, Convolvulus, Daily Courant, Gopherwood Review, Hard Ground, High Country News, Painted Hills Review, Poeisis, Poetry Motel, Prairie Dog, Red Wheelbarrow, Sanskrit, Seedhouse Magazine, SPSM&H, Trestle Creek Review,* and *Wisconsin Review.*

for Jack Ransick
1934–1989
because finally
I begin to understand

Also by Chris Ransick

A Return to Emptiness

Lost Songs & Last Chances

Asleep Beneath the Hill of Dreams

Language For the Living and the Dead

Table of Contents

Part I
Seventeen Trees

Part II
Ablation

Part III
Not Crossing the River

As any honest magician knows, true magic inheres in the ordinary, the commonplace, the everyday, the mystery of the obvious. Only petty minds and trivial souls yearn for supernatural events, incapable of perceiving that everything—everything!—within and around them is pure miracle.

—Ed Abbey

Chance and chance alone has a message for us. Everything that occurs out of necessity, everything expected, repeated day in and day out, is mute. Only chance can speak to us.

—Milan Kundera

Part I

Seventeen Trees

River House

Waste not want not she said as she
untied her shoes and tossed them,
threatless, to the corner,
fifteen miles more worn.

Can't talk about life with a straight face, she said,
someone always laughs.
Might as well be from what
plagues him as what pleases him.

And when she slid
the shirt from her shoulders, slipped into bed,
I heard a train whistle beneath
midnight crescent moon, I had to listen

to it run on down
the curve of her spine
like a track in my hand.
I saw rain run down

the window glass, same as rain falling
on wild fires burning
the forest floor and valley walls,
rain so futile and beautiful both,

falling into the river, flowing over
smooth stones in the shallows,
that river without shape
but always with direction.

And wind slapped lilac branches
on our window, gusts broke
round the house and fled again
having come through Hellgate Canyon

just to shake the blossoms
off the plum trees, brush
the chokecherry bush and
sway the crow's nest in the cottonwood.

Cottonwood

In the room where he lay with her,
August night poured through
an open window, spreading its blue ink
over their skin, hers so pale

it might be new or full,
covered with seas of dust or craters
marking impact, or the spent rings
of old infernos.

They thought themselves safe,
since no storm could pass
through the canyon and fan out
over the valley

without first rustling dry hair
of the trees, a perimeter of green
in summer, a canopy of black sticks
in November.

The gate out back would not stay closed.
There were men hidden in the weeds
that grew beyond the fence,
tramps lost along a siding

trains rarely visited. The rails
bore wheels enough
that they still gleamed in the rain,
only their edges rust red.

Sometimes he thought the knapweed
beautiful, as in July it burst a thousand
purple blooms that dipped in wind
above still-tender shoots.

But later, summer heat scorched
that back acre and grasshoppers
long as his fingers leapt
through the forest of stalks,

devouring what was not desiccated,
twirling their cruel antennae
from perches, conducting
song from the burnt throats of grass.

Too little rain, too much doubt
and trouble. He felt along her side
as she slept and found the curve
familiar but somehow smoothed,

a different hollow, a new slope
he knew was carved by time
and another's touch. The trees
shivered and touched

their leaves together, their applause
a gentle and plush rebuke.
He might have carried her to the tracks,
waking the men in the weeds as he went,

offering her passage away. He might have
carried her to the base of a tree,
hoping the rain could cleanse her,
make her whole. Instead,

he let her sleep, spent that cool hour
of night plotting to bring love back.
He knew each tree, knew the one
the crows preferred, the first

to lose its leaves in a yellow blush. He knew
when he returned, the birds would be there still.
Leaving her in bed, he dressed and shut the door
soft behind him, let the darkness

swirl around him with its
heavy, sweet scent of rain on dirt
thinking he saw the trees sway and reach
as if to hold him back.

The Hiding

1

They made love so many times
in that bare room, their bodies fighting
against something, and she never
conceived. The mattress
lay against the wood floor, the candle
she always lit wavered, measuring
the slight breeze. The closet
had no door and stood open, a mouth
gaping at them from the other world,
amused at their bones knocking together,
at the final jump of flesh
into the glistening lake where sleep
was always waiting.
He began to think of her as a wild
animal, a jet-black crow once captive
with a broken wing, now healed,
her fierce gold eyes locked on his back
as he closed the cage again for night.

2

One night he drank too much wine
and lay down in the cold grass
as the sky spun through branches above.
He remembered how to love her
but knew he'd forget by morning,
or else she'd be gone
when he awoke, his dreams receding,
their colors growing faint
before he could clutch them.
There under the tree he imagined
she was hiding in the grooved bark,
her hair blending brown to brown,
her skin a soft moss, her arms
thrown high,
abandoning birds to the sky.

The Diseased Tree

It was December, the morning chill.
The sun snagged on a crooked branch

and hung there, insistent that he wake.
Out front, a car was idling,

gunmetal gray smoke drifting across
the dead lawn, and he recalled

how weeks before a mother had strapped
her two children into their seats,

motor running in the closed garage,
and nobody found them for days.

Was it the long winter, approaching
as a bear might return to a carcass?

Was it that particular despair, the sagging
hours of daylight, the slow decay

of afternoons gone dark and cold too soon?
He listened to the car still idling

in slanting rays of sun, the yolk
gone runny where the branch broke through.

He knew that disease
had not yet consumed the tree,

sure to leaf out again in spring,
sparse green on half the limbs,

a whole side gone to rot,
and he thought of the woman

taking her keys from the dresser top,
urging the children out of their beds

and through the hall to the back door,
then out into the last morning of their lives.

He thought of her careful hands on the buckles,
fingers inserting and turning the key,

the engine leaping and settling
into its slow burn,

while outside, crows low in the limbs
shrugged off cold and waited for the children's souls.

The Moon of Popping Trees

When it got cold enough, icicles
would snap, sink into snow banks
with only a soft shush.
The moon would arrive,
a sharp disk of ice,
a taut, bright hole in the black.

It was the moon of popping trees
signaling sap to drop
one last degree and burst
the thinnest branches
still scratching at sky like they did before
the desiccated final leaf detached.

Those were the longest nights of the year,
wind rubbing invisible drums,
polishing window glass, carving
at canyons and caves, twisting
the branches that tapped the roof,
ticking like the hands of a clock.

Ghost in the Wen

Sometimes it seemed
the tree had grown a face
deliberately to peer through

their back window. The bark
on the burl had lips
where lips should be,

a mouth that might speak
if it could uncurl
its wooden grimace.

Light and shadow wrestled
on the mat of grass
atop meandering roots,

no victor but night
to close down the contest again.
What did those eyes see?

Was she moving toward him
again and again,
almost violent, her hands

frightened birds,
tangling before taking hold,
feathers batting the glass?

Theirs was one story
but there had been others:
the man who built the house

kneeling out back in the snow,
praying, as wind
blew drifts about him.

There was never any path
worn beneath that tree. No fruit
hung where early blossoms rode

on April winds until late frost.
Yet living wood grew green
beneath the bark

and late at night
the twisting wood would groan
as if to speak.

Derailment

The train had come off the tracks, a grinding heard
two miles away, the low dull sound of hollow steel

buckling and warping, wheels ripping at ties
and gravel, the sudden halt to it all.

The cold stunned him and he left his engine running,
afraid it might not start again, aware

he was the first one there amid boxcars scattered
like chunks of dark rock. First came a strange

silence, then a thing more quiet,
snow, wet and heavy,

falling on the hood of his coat. The moon
illuminated cars, all empties,

and the light made a hollow sound
so soft and pale he felt like sleep

had spilled all over the tracks,
all over the bed of stones so like his own.

Later he drove back along the rutted access road,
sliding on patches of ice

frozen in gullies and chuckholes.
In the rear view mirror the sheriff's lights

grew faint, diffusing in the February air
dry as a ghost's kiss.

A Circle of Trees

The cottonwood grew holy in the sun,
dropping gold leaves, the occasional

black feather or dry husk of bark.
Beyond the perimeter of the field

the railroad spur trembled, one of many
forgotten options, like the back door

at a bad party. She watched him
through ancient window glass

so long in the panes it had flowed,
its gentle sag revealing the sway

in his step. Neither one of them could leave,
they belonged within that circle of trees,

a canopy for stone magpies,
iridescent dust, purple and green,

sifting loose from dangling tails.
She wanted summer to end, like wanting

rain to end, a wish you always get.
He was standing in the shade, long

across grass wherever it lay,
his own shadow lost in a dark patch

the tree cast down, shreds cupped in birds' nests,
or hanging from thin twigs

till breeze separated bone from bone.
They would not blow away, she knew

though she couldn't say it aloud, sure
the truth would scare them both.

Alkali Flats

1

You hear a raspy voice,
true confessions
on the radio,
midnight anonymity.
Touch your lip with a burning stick,
in a blur it's morning.

No towns out here
on this baked plain.
Jackrabbits freeze in the headlights, flee
for scrub across the highway;
some are slaughtered
under wheels.

The pavement gleams,
swollen buttes rise up from the valley
in need of a shave.
buzzards skim their pulverized
rock and cactus skin
looking for carcasses by the road.

You are sure
you were once in love.
Your hand caressed
her hip,
a motion you would memorize.
The map you left behind

will never help.
A different route seems best this time,
perhaps through tropical places
fantastic and confused,
toucans, parrots, blue macaws
placid in the lush and threatening vines.

This desert harbors
no secrets.
Heat and light
are but one thing
in different forms in abundance
here, where lizards

lift their necks, erect
astride the yellow strip
marking the highway.
You are safe,
as long as speed propels you forward
no single sight can last.

Another dawn bleeds from the east
across the sky.
You travel west and try to ignore
wind devils whipping up
white dust from cracked
sinks and bowls.

Deranged and saddened
cowboy lyrics
come out of nowhere
just to creep down your antenna,
twitch your speakers,
tell your future.

2
In a cafe, northern Nevada, 12 noon, July,
107 degrees. Local paper reads "Man Shoots Wife."
The coffee is too bitter, cold, the water alkaline.
Waitress is as shy as girls
you knew back home, her hair an auburn
darkened place, her yellow
uniform is pressed, immaculate. The cook,
her boyfriend, watches from his cage.
She stoops to pick up from the floor
a spoon some child dropped.
Deliver me from bondage reads

the invisible tag above her breast.
You lift your eyes from the plate.
Glass separates you
from the heat
and the wavering mountain
and you whisper *this is unreal,*
whisper to yourself.

3

You travel the road that broke the back
of the snake, curled in agony
in the rear view mirror.

The desert is that dangerous.
Most travel it fast, blast through the heat
with bloodshot eyes, one sunburned arm.

Turkey vultures pick each precious
carcass, red stones bake
in empty lakes, and pocket mice

collect in the dust, hide
their young, knowing how the snake
invades and takes what she wants.

What is fear but the sound of sunrise
on a bad day? Blacktop shimmers,
sloping to the shoulders,

everything distant
begins to wriggle
like bad reception.

By night, a hundred miles
out of town, you'll follow tail lights
on curves ahead, red on seething black,

ignoring the obvious
neon signs
that nothing lasts forever.

4

It happens fast
in a falling rock zone:
one instant

eyes emerge from shadow, flash,
and nostrils flare, black hooves
pump on the road.

Slams
into hood and windshield
and is gone.

You stop
back up, but the deer
is nowhere

as you listen in the ruptured dark
to the engine click and cool.
No breeze, no moon to illuminate

tufts of fur and clots
of blood. The car
will rust where

bent metal bare of paint
marks point of impact.
As you drive on

each car approaching shines
kaleidoscopes of headlights
through the cobweb glass.

5

Suddenly you think you see a policeman behind the billboard
pulling out.

6

Once travelers chiseled a trench through sandstone cliffs
so their mules could descend to the river.
Later, miners pummeled the rock,
washed crude silver ore from veins

that sprang like hair in all directions.
Some got rich but most died of heat and disappointment,
their bones bleached and scattered with cattle bones.
Still other froze and later thawed, came back to life.

Eventually, machines peeled mountains back
like whale skin from a huge blue fin of stone, exposing
    precious metals.
They glazed the sand to glass with thermonuclear blasts.

Now, down in compacted ground,
explosions bulge, then
suck the surface in, leave scabs of science that won't heal,
that even the buzzards avoid.

7

Vast waste.
Salt crust in the basin
glimmers

where a lake once shimmered
baked by sun,
evaporating.

Highways have since
laced the snow-white
flats, black

shoestring lanes
knotting up in
desert towns and interchanges.

At night the heat
floats back up sky,
perimeter fences snag the countless

bulbous tumbleweeds
blown in from places
where plants can live.

Nothing grows on alkali flats,
no plants no towns no dreams,
just mineral crystals,

bitter taste,
salt crust,
vast waste.

Black Branches

On a raw November afternoon,
he first noticed the craggy limbs
stunted by hard Montana winters.

The old man had said
the tree wasn't dead;
it bore fruit every year

until bad pruning drove it down,
but you'll see buds next spring.
All winter he watched black branches

bob and dance in wind, the uppermost
just past his reach,
and furthest from the warm wood heart.

In February, cold pressed dry turf down
and hovered, dulling the sun in a sky
of grey skin, and he recalled

the woman who grew cherries
near the lake. She said bad winters
doubled the yield, as though

the trees sensed death
traveling inward through their roots
and so burst out in fruit.

And so it was.
In May the twisted limbs
hung thick with blooms.

The Avenue of Dying Palms

1

It's the saddest tree, with its bad posture,
scales, and loose hair. It casts narrow shade,
thin straps across the avenue to hold asphalt

in place during quakes. The palms lash
during January's rains, when torrents
fall like punishment

against the houses, when waves rise
in frothy peaks, chaotic and angry,
scraping back the beach until its bones lie

exposed, the black-veined rocks,
the pitiful fields of split sand dollars,
the smooth polished chips of green glass.

2

He brought her here, to the avenue
of dying palms, so she could see the moon
light the wet, salty air as with phosphor,

so she might believe his story of how
one night a sea mammal beached
beside the jetty, exhausted.

He heard a moaning, its voice
like the slow complaint of an old woman
calling from another room.

It came from the water to lie on that cool,
receding layer of silk
waves spread on sand before retreating.

That night he shared with her,
no creature came ashore. The constant lapping
on the rocks lulled them both,

and she slept briefly, her hand
curled in his, her breast rising beneath
the delicate curve of her shirt.

He did not wake her. It was good
to watch her sleep, at rest in a place
without defenses or charms against pain.

3

He had seen films of giant timber
falling to earth, the great crash of branches
and the croak of rending wood.

Still, he never imagined a palm
vulnerable, never thought of how a crew might arrive
early one Tuesday, unload the equipment

and stand around smoking, trying to plot
the fall line. What cruel saws, what a terrible noise,
teeth biting into the slender trunk.

It takes no time at all to fell a palm. The trunk
is thin as a man's torso, the wood soft and pulpy.
And when it falls, it falls right where they plan.

Accusations

Mostly it was whispering, a ghost
with tongue stuck in his throat

trying to speak through cottonwood trees,
the moonlight shredded by

surging wind. No one understood
the language, ancient and composed

of soft slashes and bruises,
words that broke and spilled from their centers

new words, a long sentence saying nothing
and everything. Limbs flailed and leaves

tore off, too early for autumn.
As he walked the avenue, dragging

his secrets, he didn't hear the voice
so subtle it enveloped him and tossed

his hair. The sidewalk cracks
spelled cryptic oaths before his eyes,

and crows scolded him for hiding,
their caws reporting the crime.

There will be no more safety, a voice said,
and then the wind obscured the voice.

The dry grass, bent with August heat,
shivered, rustled, and answered.

Just Dawn

The thinnest snow lay on the earth
and stars snagged on the cottonwoods.
They held each other, sharing breath

and never heard the chinook blow
nor did they see the sun's first light,
though both had dreams of melting snow.

They slept so deep throughout the night
they woke and could no longer say
which one was wrong, which one was right.

They walked the morning warmth away
and knew that spring had come to stay.

The Five Year Shirt

1

She sits in the chair by the window,
waiting for crows to swim down the sky,
their shadows sudden darkness on grass,
and she sews the five year shirt.

Even the cloth draped over her hands
is moving in the light as curtains move
in wind just strong enough to press through
window screens, chasing July heat.

In the other room, black and white photos
come to life, time moves backward,
faces of old women grow tumescent,
fingers on the hands of old men stretch.

2

Another winter comes,
brittle branches popping

in the orchard,
sap finally frozen.

Even the music on the radio
billows like cold smoke

from speakers as she
raises the blinds for light

and it tangles
coming through the slats,

laying knotted strands across
fabric of the five year shirt.

3

Wind turns the trees to mimes,
mimics the sound of feet
shuffling on floorboards of empty rooms
above where they lie.

He dreams of the man whose heart caved in,
sees him writhe on the kitchen floor,
pain twisting bones and blue light pouring
from a hole in the sky.

Across the field the full moon loves,
new snow covers his prints.
Then the sound of a coyote yapping,
tight and sharp, at shadows.

4

By now the shirt has seams.
She sews the hem line in her dreams

and when she wakes she pulls the pins
out of the cloth, forgetting none.

5

It's the five year shirt.
It takes that long to sew because
the thread is invisible.

And the shirt lies like a bruise
on the tabletop,
waiting for his body to fill it.

Caw

He saw the crows had wings so black,
even at night their shapes
left holes between stars,
darker than the vacant water of lakes
high in alpine bowls.

At noon, he saw the crows as black knives
slicing sunlight and he prayed for them to leave.
He knew a rifle could scatter feathers, muscles,
hollow bones, but their magic was
his wish for that very death.

At night the crows perched outside his room
as though tending his dreams
like a nest of their own black eggs,
hunched on the limbs, calling out, naming
the stones of fear he'd hoped to hide.

Tree of Lies

Under the tree that hung over the river
he read her letters again, the last time
words would spill so carelessly
from her hands into his, the last time
he would imagine her shadow
reversed in the moonlight and hiding
behind thick cottonwood trunks
on the far bank. Hers was never
a sure caress, he could relinquish
its pleasure like some relinquish
pain, willingly but aware of loss.
The moon rose low, bridge girders
a strange geometry above willows
bent to cold water like Flathead women
bathing in high summer heat.
Her letters floated downstream,
the ink finally loosened and free
to dissolve its brief meanings.
The trees kept the secret,
and he left them to their silence,
his head full of betrayal, a lover
of bone and muscle, blood and heat,
waiting to reclaim him.
There was nothing to do but return home,
unlock the door, go in, undress, lie down,
let the breeze leap the sill and wash them both
as the river does stones
that have lain together so long
and will lie still longer,
caressed by trout and currents
until smooth as skin.

Morning After a Bitter Year

He fixed her breakfast as he always had,
a black plate flanked by knife and fork, a cup

for tea, a red cloth napkin in a ring.
The canyon east of town had burned

all night and morning sun blew amber breath
through the smoke. The charred stumps

on the shoulders of rock
would smolder for seven days above

the river, as usual, escaping
forever toward its rendezvous.

You would have thought them older,
sitting as they did in silence, eating

in silence like the long-married,
remembering the residue of many mornings,

and as they ate a ghost slid out
through the pane behind her,

tangling in the drapes a moment,
aware the haunting was through.

Part II

Ablation

Premonition

In the car accident,
the man's blue car speeds
toward my wife and children,
driving into the intersection.

Relax, it's an illusion, I tell myself,
see what happens. Maybe they'll fly up
through open windows, hand in hand,
to escape the blue car.

But later, I see real skid marks on the street,
sidewinding toward the median,
and also the bent signpost,
the scattered glass and plastic.

Later, in the hospital
I tell her: just two days ago
I had a premonition,
an impossible coincidence,

as you backed out of the driveway,
past purple blooms on the clematis,
and you were singing with the kids
a nonsense rhyme, fallen elm twigs crackling

under the tires, twilight
and lightning backlighting
the rough bruises of a storm cloud
sliding northeast.

In a trick of the sun and shade I thought
I saw our car was dented,
bashed in on the driver's side,
just a trick of sun and shade.

On the way home I walk along
a row of trees, slats of light falling
on rich green grass, remembering
the words to their song,

where everything is contrary,
where forward motion takes you backward,
where time is not in line,
and lines hold nothing in.

Laura's Garden

I might walk through your garden
on a winter's day, the nectarine bough
that brushed my ear on summer nights
now loosed of its burden, unbowed,
and bare above me,

the central California sky
shedding a mist that might be rain
if this were not a dream
and I were not the maker of that dream,
though of course I am, you understand.

Gardens go empty, even where
the myth of perpetual growth
overlooks failed cabbage crops of locals
and the burnt rice fields, bisected
by crazy tractor trails. Crops do fail

and gardens go empty. They must
so we can imagine new designs:
images of bulbous squash trembling
under the dark green foliage
August insists upon.

Look, the soil's full of holes and swimming
with small live things as we speak.
The chickens are skirting the raspberry stalks
clucking, strutting, evacuating,
and the seeds of neglected tomatoes

are plotting to volunteer. If I did
walk through your garden again,
I'd remember things like the slow hum humming
of a hot June evening, the damn bent spoon
you use to serve your food,

and the poster of the woman
washing herself at the sink. This
is a friendly haunting, my memory
of living where you live, strolling barefoot
past scattered English walnuts,

attempting to discern which pepper burns
and which is sweet. Forgive me for leaving.
I hope that everything grows
the way it should. I hope those unusual flowers,
blue and pale, pop up through the grass.

Putah Creek Sonnets

I Go Swimming at Putah Creek

The hot dry wind through car windows has blown
my hair into a scarecrow's yellow wig
of straw, hand on wheel a five-fingered fig,
and each eyeball a red-veined flower grown
in a parched arroyo. The cold creek snakes
green through tan hills. Are the blue oaks weeping
in wicked sun still hours from slipping
through a notch in the Vacas? Each tree quakes
as I undress, dust blooms around my feet,
mixes with sweat, one mud bead forms and drips.
A paintbrush on the bank waves its red tips.
Lake Berryessa's bottom, in such heat,
still dribbles frigid water down rock.
I plunge from the gnarled tree limb, skin in shock.

I Take the Kids to Putah Creek in Winter

She only barely walks, he barely talks
in sentences, a frothy, tumbled fall
of words that splashes, floods the rounded rocks
in my ears. He grabs the winter weeds, tall
and brittle, by their stalks and yanks them out,
swishes them in the creek, sprays his sister
with green drops. Does the timbre of her shout
make the fog-shy sun slip even faster
for the shadows solstice folds into slopes
of coastal hills? Her translucent hair flies
in the breeze, she grips dark and twisted ropes
of bark and stares at me, at water, eyes
unsure. When we rest in the grass, we drift;
child, child, father, each of us in our craft.

We Watch the Perseids from Cold Canyon

We lie on the Mexican blanket, spread
over brickle bush and coyote brush.
Though stars make no sound, we tell him, "Hush,
and listen for the shooting stars." His head
swivels, as late cicadas scratch their songs
for later lovers in the canyon oaks.
The sky, still blue, fades black and one star pokes
out to the east, but doesn't fall. The prongs
of constellations we don't know arch lights
toward the belt of Perseus, who flings
his meteors to earth on August nights,
and while the lonely last cicada sings,
a burning rock unlaces in the sky,
orange heart breaking, this its final try.

Walking Into the Storm

It'll rain, I say,
maybe hard
if you go now. I know,

she says, I know but
we've all got our raincoats and
shade trees

line the way.
So I watch her pack
the children into a

two-seat stroller
while coolness rushes
through the open door

into our house,
a ripe cool thick
as storm clouds.

The curious dark
of this morning feels
anticipatory,

an electric thirst
buzzing from the upthrust
summer fields, stripped

of crops
ignored by blades
and the gentle touch of rain.

She says goodbye; our son
chips in his own
goodbye an octave

higher. Our tiny girl
a silent
creamy sculpture,

absorbs all.
The door closes
and they're gone.

I rush to the window,
not wanting them to go.
Wait, I think, wait

for Dad. But there they are
already down the street,
the cool wind turned

by now to chill,
her brown hair
blown back from her face

and sky
already lowering
its heavy burden down.

If I Were You and You Were Me
and We Were Also Them

We'd buy the smallest house you've ever seen,
a fixerupper with a tiny porch
that tilts, can't hold a couch,
garage paint peeling

in the white hot sun,
the whole frame crouched
along a skinny driveway, a thick blue oak
casting its stub of shade

on a basketball court
with too low hoop, a trap of bikes
by the back steps. If I were you
and you were me and we were also them,

we'd drive home on a dirt back road
crossed by dazed cattle, an occasional bird's
dark armspan falling through the orchard
canopy, ticking the waxy leaves.

Even if the trees burned like rags
and tossed up a hill of ash,
we'd harvest the last bushel of limes
or bag of black walnuts from a hidden tree,

we'd slip into the river, green and
cold, and float like sticks, nudging
rocks and bobbing, our skin
growing pale and touch in the cold.

If I were you and you were me, sifting
through our attic of debris, we'd find
the cedar chest sill exhales its musk
when we lift the lid and tug

each secret from its stem. If we were them
we'd never have to worry about us,
we'd talk until our tongues spilled in disgust,
we'd eat until we bent our forks and spoons

or wore them down to nubbins on our food.
Such fantasies are wasted—we're in luck:
it never matters what we say or do,
we always seem to end up me and you.

In the Blackberry Bushes

Let's go down in the blackberry bushes,
where thorny stalks plunge out of the loam
along the path through the woods behind
the house where Mr. Bergen died,
breastbone pressing his paper lungs down.
Not even the smell of new cut grass
could rouse him at last, not even the scent
of blackberries bleeding in the shade
could rouse him, not even the faint sting
of spearmint crushed underfoot.
Let's go down in the blackberry bushes
till our arms are tattooed with scratches.
We'll purple our palms with fat fruit,
tossing back our heads, drinking deep
from blue summer evening as light fails
and the great maple tree wears the first
red tinges on its leaves, hanging over
the huge split rock, granite
damp with a moss patina, woods resounding
with the shouts of children, the swish
of cars on a distant street, the shriek
of Canada jays raiding in the trees.
Let's go down in the blackberry bushes,
sleep is coming soon, the call to home
and then sleep, so let's go deep
where color can stain us and flavor fill us.

Trainride Lengthwise California

Magpies wait in the waist-high corn for dawn,
crows rest in the tops of palms
lilting over tomato rows. The train leaves
anyway, sprints past indigenous

marshes, grassland, skims
red mud of desiccated pools
past brown tufts of tule, tule
past the beat carcasses of cars.

Jackrabbit, stay a minute, but it darts
from the track. A catatonic pheasant stands
stiff by an abandoned boat,
a grey wood hull that long since

relaxed form and fell to frowning.
Passengers scan the Vacas, southwest
to the coastal mountains, brim
of a steaming cup of fog.

We are leaving, not coming back
past the math of fence slats
clumped like musical notes. Eucalyptus
slowly slough long strips of bark

and rain a rain of husky seeds
as the breeze does its thing, gets
in the feather ends of pampas grass
and shimmies. A pair of hawks tilt

one wing, then the next, and rise
in thermal drafts above Salinas.
Mothballed shops in a backwater bay
rust, rust in their moorings

their dank rooms and dark interiors
each as good as a nightmare.
For this much we are grateful:
for the train, listing, and clacking,

dropping bass notes, thumps
on the Earth's acoustic crust.
The drunks three seats ahead
got sloppy long before Lompoc

and have begun to curse, young drunks
old enough at last to have bad luck.
By Santa Barbara one has found
his snore, the others, magazines.

The train carves past a burned out
Santa Barbara store, black melted lumps
of tires, sculptures of a fool who tossed
his cigarette on a patch of weeds.

A hundred homes have turned charcoal blots,
soot spores dribbling up
along with smoke. The train
is Union Station bound. L.A.'s about to combust

in an orange light, its acrid halitosis
at last approaching critical mass.
We penetrate miles of well-developed
real estate, green perfect parks tucked

grudgingly under overpass or
spread across false folds of old landfills
where conning towers' spread-legged stances
tempt kids' kites and send out this

white noise: buzzzuzzzz.
Gridwork lights arise, the train
threads the electric patch
below Chavez Ravine's corona

down to the stopping place.
We exit, leave our metal snakeskin
shed on the tracks, and wish
for wings or fins or faster legs.

Hills Like Breakers

For Dean

If I lived in the valley all my life,
the low brown hills advancing over cropland
every night like waves upon a furrowed beach,

I might wake some morning wet,
a salty rock shellacked with gritty sand,
sea moss in my crevasses, anemones

suckered to my open palms, mouth hairs
wooing the dun snails in, and everywhere
soft whisperings for another wave.

But I was just a visitor who slept
a thousand nights with that low rumbling
of hills like breakers in my ears,

thinking of traffic on the never-vacant
highway made that sound. So it was
I never saw the gold grass spill,

never saw slow motions in the hills,
except for simple shivers rippling
up arroyos on hot afternoons.

Not even moonlight, buttering
the town, the fields, the hills,
made ocean out of them or beach of us.

But you of the barnacle's stationary peace,
have always seen those low round hills as waves,
pacific, arched to wash across the flat land

without rush and seep into the soil,
leaving bits of shell and skeleton,
and long green drapes of kelp upon the streets.

If We Look Into Her Eyes

If we look into her eyes we see
blue fish swimming in a bowl, round each other,

flitting as though chased, or else we see
clouds gathering, dark blooms.

If we look into her eyes we see
she's looking away, at a moth

in a dance that looks to us like chaos
but to her is ballet in air.

If we look into her eyes we see
the black discs first, the sharp

outline into which our light goes,
not to escape in a lifetime.

Letter From My Father in Shangri La

I am writing on this beautiful day because
the pain is finally gone. My brain is healed
from sitting in the silver rain, under eucalyptus,
from swimming in the pale green rivers that spill
shallow and warm from the hills.

I got you a shirt from a local shop.
It's exotic, big breast pockets,
gold dragons embroidered on collar and sleeve.
I think you'll like it, though I can't send it,
for obvious reasons.

At dawn, the light here is fantastic
and it's always 72 degrees at noon,
though some nights brisk wind blows
and the trees will creak, a limb may break.

All our disagreements now are past.
I know when you lay your children down,
they bury their faces in the crook of your neck,
their bodies fully prepared to dream.

There's nothing I can do to help you now
but say believe in what you do and do it well.
This letter is my last, though you may get
a rush of color some nights as you drift off
into sleep, and that is me.

Three Poems for Sleep

son's hurried footsteps
down the hall toward our bed
small, cold feet on thigh

rushing wind outside
whipsaw limbs of elm and ash
cut starlight to shreds

November, new snow
wet, brown leaf on hardwood floor
her breathing softens

Dead People Poems

1. Dead People Watch the Softball Game

Even as they sit, the dry brown grass
unbent by their bodies and lilting in breeze,
mosquitoes swirling through their curious
lack of scent, the dead people scratch
itches they once had and fold their arms
over their knees, rest their chins,
watch the smooth white ball as it spins
out of the pitcher's hand in an arc
over the dirt, falling out of space
toward the batter uncoiling from his crouch,
bat beginning to loop past hip, narrowly
missing the catcher's mitt, umpire's
black cloth catching shadow
in folds, infielders up on their toes and leaning
inward toward the action, gloved hands
out and splayed, throwing hands fisted,
outfielders tensed except for right field,
where the slumped stance and distracted
glance suits a forgotten teammate.

The dead hang about this field, hooking
fingers through the chain link on hot afternoons
when all the players are off to jobs and home,
pale white sunshine leaking through
translucent clouds and the imprecise
boundaries of their wispy bodies, a knot
of them gathered near the closed concession,
sucking on empty Cokes and gnawing
on the tops of discarded candy wrappers,
lips supple and weightless, immaterial teeth
whose cavities are twice nothingness,
clicking in the silence of dust and dugouts,
even as the maintenance man arrives
to chalk the lines from home plate to fence
and drops his smoking cigarette butt
through a pair of open hands.

2. Dead People Dance in a Wet Spring Snowfall

It starts as rain, a glaze on the supermarket
parking lot. Down avenues, cars grow slick
and tense dogs bark at back doors hoping,

hoping to be let in. Dust slides shut over western
peaks, a dark bleach spreading everywhere,
chilling the hot narrow stems of seedlings.

The dead people huddle beneath suburban eaves,
remembering to shiver, gently, and then
to stamp their feet in silence, without splash.

The temperature licks at their bare, invisible
necks. The first sheet of grey snow
goes to slush on bushes, buds,

and the glass sidewalk, and out they come
to dance, to open their arms wide
and let the snowflakes swirl down through

the tops of their heads. Before morning
the wet white town will smother streets
and snap thick branches from trees.

For now the dead are pleased to thrash
on the perfect snow of sloping lawns,
to make angels without the weight

of bodies. Their hands scoop through
the wet spring snow, leaving no
impression. Neighborhood cats

lurk beneath cars and behind the trunks
of cottonwoods, watching the dead people
lift and let fall their arms in rhythm,

singing for cold and the perfect pull
of gravity that draws this moisture down
on the city still in temporary sleep.

3. *The Newly Dead See Their Frame House Sold*

The real estate agent jingles the ring
of keys, soft chimes moistening
the June afternoon just loud enough
to wake the dead. She's at the sewing machine,
fingers resting on uncut cloth and
dipping in the jar of buttons. He's
in the garage, plucking the belt
on the generator as though it were
the D-sting of a double-bass.

A young couple enters, clean kids
fresh from jobs downtown, creases
instead of backbones, wallets
thick with plastic, children still
sealed away in zygote heaven,
each one awaiting its rude collision.
They step inside behind the salesman
who says with a sniff, "There's been a death."

She sighs a breath so light, even the dust
frosting the surface of the black flywheel
remains at rest. She follows them from
room to room, draping herself across
the furniture, cringing when lookers flush
the rust water out of the bowl, remembering
as they crack the pantry door, the beets,
beans, and applesauce she meant to eat
still neatly canned and stacked, and the freezer
packed with bags of loganberries, sour
cherries. The old dead
hug again in the kitchen as
the young couple pass through their arms.

The screen door slams. The yard
flames, but only to their eyes; to the young man
it's just grass he'll need to cut. Poppies,
shorn of black and orange petals, crane
their necks for a look, the baubles bowing

to no particular breeze. The peach trees,
having outlived gentle pruning,
will not bear this year. At the window,
the dead people disappear, the stale air
turns to mint and pine, the stairwell
creaks a couple times, the front door
doesn't budge.

4. The Dead Go to Church

It's in that hour, the dead time of morning before
dawn, when aisle stones ache for knees of supplicants
who yet writhe fiercely in their beds, still awash
in pastel wisps of deepening dreams.
Even the priest is dreaming, yes, his hands
about the throat of a suicide, choking, choking
the devil forth. It's then the pipe organ moans
so softly in minor key, pigeons roosting in the bell tower
open their eyes but don't take flight. Great slabs
of stone atop forgotten graves glow blue-green
under snow and the faithful float again into garments of
black and white, bibles and hymnals
opening silently to pages that can't be read.
The oak pews won't creak beneath this
misty congregation; their sins were long ago
and can't be shrived, their prayers are filaments
of smoke that spin down and disappear
into gaps between stones. A phantom prelate
mounts the pulpit, pausing so long
even the dead forget eternity and grow
restless, the few unfortunate children fidgeting
as though Jesus were calling them to the
pancake breakfast, to pools of sweet syrup
their tongues can never taste. Instead,
a sermon: What does it profit a dead man
if he rise in the night and gaineth the whole world
but can't locate the shrine of his departed soul?
This Mass of specters goes on too long,
just to be realistic. The altar boys will not
remove their frowns, the nuns, actually improved
by death, cluster in a front pew, remembering
rulers and glue, sated by a celibacy easier to abide
in bodies without heat. Cool grey coins strike
collection plates without a sound. A stray ray of sun
passes first through purples in the stained-glass,
blowing its hue into vapor, signaling

the service is complete. The dead shuffle their feet
and head for the exits, some shaking the hand
of the priest. Bones beckon them back
to lie and ruminate on parables they couldn't
grasp in life but which now have become so clear.

5. *The Dead Ski Vail*

Moguls grow thin ice upon their humps,
the troughs packed hard, the temperature
falling a degree a minute until
firs shiver and drop their bough-loads.

Dead skiers, mere suggestions of
magenta and peach jackets, emerge from
the aspens, shadows betrayed by twilight,
to slash down the vacant runs

as a phantom chair lift fades into view.
The wash of their skis paints slopes
with phosphor spray. None will fall,
gliding as they do an inch above the snow,

weightless, without momentum, synchronized.
They flow the gaps between thick pines
through which no living skier could squeeze,
then dip and weave among dark moguls.

At the bottom, there is no line for the
chair lift that doesn't exist. They get right on,
assisted by pale operators obviously stoned
and bored to death with death. It's a long ride

to the top but the night is young, there's time.
The moon's pocked disc throws cold light as
blue-black flakes float through these shades,
covering the tracks they never make.

6. Dead People Go to Night School

The classroom gradually empties of light.
A late summer evening sun
drapes sharp shadows over empty chairs,
rolls lines into corners and angles.

The dead will enter this room first,
before the early student arrives
with her cup of coffee and doughnut
from the vending machines.

They will arrive before her,
following the janitor who stoops
and mumbles, who returns the waste can
to a landscape of receptacles.

The plastic seats will still conform
to their insubstantial spines.
In silence and fading light they'll see
weird formulas churning across the board,

abandoned scribblings of an afternoon
chemistry class, the runes obscure,
the conclusions the same: combine
these things this way for that result.

But they know there is nothing to learn after death
and too much to learn before.
Having come this far the dead
recall how truths could convulse

on the lips and refuse delivery,
a temporary muteness, when they had lips
and tongues, real lungs that moved air
when wisdom joined mystery.

They stay this night in the room
until the early student comes, just
as they knew she would, cool tubes
overheard banishing at her command

the twilight that was there.
They stay until the room is full,
until the uncombed professor deposits
his heavy book on the table

and greets the class, their song of chatter
withering, their bodies heavy in the chairs.
The dead line up in the back, where fluorescence
and twilight meet through the blinds of their ribs.

They stay though they know that tonight is *Hamlet*,
though they know every time the play is read
the Prince must murder Polonius
in error, must cast off Ophelia

who must herself descend to the river
and there soak her dress till it drags her down.
This play they know by hearts
they once had, so they stay just until

Hamlet's father lurches through the door,
his body clearly the same as theirs,
and beckons them out to the battlements,
back home in the chilling night.

In the *Maltese Falcoln*, Humphrey Bogart

Rolls himself a cigarette, worries only briefly
about his murdered partner, uses the phone
often, greets the police lieutenant as if
he doesn't understand
women, or the crime. Bogart
sends the widow away, has his partner's name

scraped from the door. The widow asks him
to be kind, the client
to be generous, the secretary
rolls him a cigarette and lights it, legs crossed as she
sits on the desk. The client
asks again, this time for patience. Bogart

asks for money. He has none of the things
they seek; even the gunman who asks for
information gets none. When his bag of tobacco gets low,
the fat man hands him cigars; not once,
but twice, and lights them. Everyone pours drinks
from decanters, the liquor amber

in a black and white way. Finally,
Bogart succumbs to a mickey, spins and slumps;
the punk with the heater
kicks him in the ribs for kicks. Upon reviving, Bogart
uses the phone again. The bird
turns up, wrapped in newspaper,
delivered by a dying man.

Bogart washes his hands. Blood
swirls down the sink. The bird is lead
and he knows it. The crooks are anxious
to unwrap it and he knows it. Afterward,
the client asks for mercy and he has none.
The crooks have wasted 17 years.

Bogart lights a cigarette.

The Rugby Girls

Wouldn't you like to wrestle with the rugby girls,
tussle their rough-ribbed bodies in the scrum,
where stiff spine resists spine as they unfurl,
thrown ecstatically to the grit till black bruises bloom.

Tussling rough-ribbed bodies buck in the scrum,
cough the ball up, toss it back. See the lateral spill
down chains of sweaty hands, down sidelines rumbling,
the team intent, with gritted teeth, to make the goal.

They cough it up and curse, toss it back, the handoff spills
and little clots of mud flip up behind their cleats.
Bodies thud, grind gritted teeth, and head for goal.

Little clots of mud flip up behind her cleats
as she cuts to left, fakes right, and lowers down
her shoulders, an elbow to the breast like lead
on flesh, absorbing shock when bones hit ground.

They run, cut left, fake right, big one goes down.
Clean sideline boys with beer breath and short hair
flinch when feminine flesh and bone hit ground.
Such offense, defense, now is all they share.

When spine resisting spine does its slow unfurl
don't they long, like you, to wrestle with the rugby girls?

The Fat Boy Rollerskates Home

Along an L.A. side street, pavement cracked
as if by silent temblors in the night,
the fat boy navigates in evening light.
He's rollerskating home, his backpack packed
so tight he seems a soldier from some war,
a grunt who's left to carry all he owns
back from the front, the fractured, ashy bones
of friends who learned what they were fighting for.
His skates catch in the cracks, his face streams sweat,
the dusty eucalyptus rain down seed,
like tiny rocks his progress they impede.
He glances skyward, eyes grown desperate,
and scans the ochre air above the street
where sooty angels hover in the heat.

Death Suite

1. Death is a Mailman

who comes to you
in the afternoon with a letter you don't want,
postage due, certified, your name and address
unmistakably on the front.
He hands you his pen and says, "Sign."

Death walks the sidewalks with amazing grace,
blue uniform shorts creased and snug, a smile
impossibly white. He looks like a civil servant should.
The dogs that chase him chomp
their teeth on empty air.

Death is a mailman you don't know.
He'll bring you junk mail, circulars,
bright advertisements, bills, debris
from the dead letter office. Don't shake his grizzled
hand in the glaring sun,

in the afternoon, on your front porch,
when mailboxes ache with emptiness,
when sinister packages lurk in his
shadowy bag. One of the letters he hands you
could be an invitation.

2. Death is a Third Baseman

who throws the ball to you
at first base, where you stand with your glove poised
and ready to catch, and you know you must not
drop the ball, the damn ball,
coming your way as if on a clothesline. Death

caught the ball on a Sunday hop, effortlessly
he bent at the knee, turned to the left
in a perfect pivot, scooping air inside
his leathered hand
and turned again

to face you.
His uniform is caked with mud, the baseball
very white. Red seams come out of his hand
on a spiral, spinning clockwise, a screwball drifting
just to your left and up.

But you're not up to bat now; you must catch
his toss. It's the third out of the last inning
of a rain-shortened playoff game. You'll miss
the Series, though your team will play
and wear black armbands for you.

3. Death is a Waitress

who brings you a menu, a colorful
menu with just one entrée. She hands
the plastic-coated thing to you, seated
in the smoking section.
You ask for a cocktail; she just shakes her head,

hand on ample hip, and clicks her gum
through pale blue lips. Each patron
of the place looks nervous, each
stabs at the dish in front of him with fork
or spoon or knife. It's life

they want to eat, just one more bite,
and possibly dessert: retirement cookies
or a slice of golf vacation pie. No dice.
The waitress, she can wait forever.
Phantom cooks amid black pots and pans

will flip and sizzle burgers in the back
all night at her command.
She doesn't have to write your order down,
or bring your check. She doesn't count on you
to leave a tip.

4. Death is a Lover

who comes to you
in the morning, in your bed, when your eyes are poor
and adjusting to light, when the night still spits
its wet scent into the air, when streets steam
and streetlights flicker, then go out. Death

lifts the covers from you, slips beside
and takes your hand. So cold
is her skin you take a deeper breath, release
each of your dreams from its thin strand,
knowing you soon will wake.

Death is a lover you haven't met.
She brings you something to drink; don't drink it
until you know her better, can describe
her blonde and silky hair to strangers
well enough to scare them.

She comes in the morning
of your life, before you're ready. Her hands
so graceful as she holds you, finding their way
inside your body with a pain
too hard and fine to explain.

Three Feet Tall

By morning's measurement, she's three feet tall,
standing straight up with her smooth dolphin back,
with the disks of her heels, soft-fleshed but thick,
jammed against baseboard of warped kitchen wall.
The pale crown of her head fits in my palm
with gentle pressure and I feel heels rise,
reach for that extra quarter inch of size;
the camera in my mind unspools its film.
She's three feet tall, little woman in blue.
Strawberry jam stains the crease of her smile.
She arrives new each day, as children will,
with yawning puddles of mud to march through.
I hold her still and mark her three feet tall;
she darts off, leaves just the mark on the wall.

The Bearded Woman Walks By

The sun is bright on the smudged glass.
Heat breathes over the coffee cup,

lifting steam out by its vanished end,
a wisp dancing over the stained tablecloth.

The waitress brings eggs, edges
tinted with grease, and a heap of fries.

Snatching the check from her belt
she smiles, flips it face down, and is gone.

Outside, a bus delivers its payload
of beat citizens: a blind man exits,

hits shins on the splintered wood bench
and lurches out into the empty lane,

brown fumes billowing round him.
Out of nowhere, shuffling through glare

with thirty stiff red whiskers curved
down over her chin, the bearded woman

traverses against the light. The bus
waits until she's past, driver

staring through his flat windshield.
A businesswoman in a white sedan

taps her fingers on the dash.
This spring morning, the birds

have grown giddy, chasing each other
in flashing arcs from precipice to

telephone wire, circling over
nature's freaks, those navigating asphalt,

those eating breakfast in a shaft of sun,
toast, jam, hot black coffee.

Ablation

The children appear at the door in pajamas
smelling of bath, wet hair in my face.

I hold their still very small-boned hands,
skin newer than mine, less coarse, their necks

and wrists supple, soft arms around my neck.
Outside, when heavy snow slid down strings

and melted away, I carried them both
from the car over grey sheets on the grass,

their bodies slack and heavier,
heavier in my arms than days before.

I hold them just a moment, tents of energy
vibrating against my chest, released

and bounding up the steps, hands out
for balance, but they might be gliding.

Hospital Poem

This nurse's hands are small.
She lifts my arm and lets it fall
back into the nest of sheets.

In the cool half-light I dream
of a woman next door, of her muffled scream
soothed by the swish of people passing

beyond the perimeter of my view,
all through the slick-tile halls, all through
floors of right angles and intersections,

to and from rooms of lancing pain
where green lines sway like stalks of grain,
show video visions of major organs

moved by gentle respiration,
bone-hinged bodies, fine integration
of a hundred systems.

Back in my room the equipment hums,
again in the dark, again she comes,
a blur against the blue-grey wall,

and again her hands are small and warm.
She covers my body against all harm
and so warms the feet I cannot reach.

She taps into and fills a vein
with liquid light and salty rain,
she weaves away, away and leaves

through the portal of an empty wall
as my shoulders tilt back and begin to fall,
a snowflake afloat in moonless night.

The Things We Couldn't Explain

1

It started in the kitchen, the footsteps
from underneath, as if the floor were
walked by the resident

of a second, invisible house,
its seams and surfaces
the opposite of ours.

I wouldn't say it frightened us,
only that we became aware
we'd deceived ourselves till then.

2

What would you say if a child appeared
in your hallway, when the light was dim
and her eyes shone

but her frame was mere suggestion?
What if she beckoned you, a wrist
supple and thin, immaterial

but irresistible, a grey scarf
lifted by the breeze, though there was
no breeze? What would you say to her

to explain death, her presence
once real but brief, now turned
to this? Would you speak to her at all?

I think you would not. The sight of her
standing there, the slow motions,
the face you can't quite see

a mask in the shadows, all this
would silence you, just the dull tick
of a clock somewhere

to rouse you from the vision
turned to vapor
and receding.

3

Yesterday, a terrific wind
swept round the house, roughly tossing
the limbs of trees, swirling seed
and dust in funnels, visible as
the churning torsos of doomed men.
Pebbles clattered against the door,
fresh sprouted leaves tore free
and the squirrels clung to
corrugated bark as birds dove low.
It lasted half a minute, passing
with a shred of murky cloud
that dangled virga from its tail,
a cruel promise in a drought year.

4

In the room
directly behind her

she heard a woman speak and felt
strands of a web

drawn across her face,
her skin sensing warmth

as if someone stood near,
someone whose body was fevered.

5

These were things we couldn't explain.
When in evening light bent to gold
by atmosphere a moth crawled up

the kitchen wall, I looked away
but from the corner of my eye,
I saw it curl into a ribbon of soot.

Dealey Plaza, Dallas, November 1993

Cars keep coming
down the slope
toward signs that read "Airport"

and "Interstate."
No X marks the blacktop,
of course no blood remains.

A man selling newspapers,
JFK Today News,
shadows me over the grassy knoll,

wanting my dollar
but it's the dead
who will buy him lunch.

Construction workers dig at the dirt
but no ghosts fly up
from the tips of their shovels,

shrieking, proclaiming
the guilt
only assassins know.

What are they building
or excavating?
Things were torn down here.

Then one worker says,
"Can't dig through these
goddamn roots.

It's supposed to be a
grassy knoll,
not a rooty knoll,"

and he curses again,
the trees shaking pigeons
out of their hair.

They say Jackie
climbed over the seat
to escape,

to seek shelter
from the Secret Service man,
to get out of the rain.

Her terrible fear
must have spilled everywhere,
like noon sun in November will,

and 30 years later
it still drips off the bushes
and the concrete steps,

invisible to these people
who have come to prod the soft holes
history left in this place.

And I came, too,
who knew nothing on that day
except my mother's breast

and how my mouth filled
with bitter milk.
I knew nothing else,

not Texas, not bullets
not Cuba or Kruschev,
my own death more distant

than it would ever be.
Now I'm under the 6th floor window
listening to the newspaper man

talk trivia, conspiracy
to a customer, who fishes
in his pocket for bills.

Cars keep passing the spot,
fenders and windshields
rippling as though liquid

and I half expect the motorcade
heading north on Houston,
turning on Elm and slowing,

everyone smiling for the last time ever
and squinting into the light,
cameras clicking and whirring.

Ten Things About a Mandolin

After two beers, it sounds better; after three, worse.

Until you learn to play slow and soft, you are a novice.

Play outdoors, in the summer, for full effect.

Don't trade your mandolin for anything, not even a _____.

Spruce, maple, ebony, mahogany.

Find a good guitarist.

Children may dance about while you play. Then you will not want to st

Play the old songs with authors unknown.

Sing your favorite song while restringing the mandolin.

There is never enough time, not for anything.

The Giant Icicle

Really, it's a ladder to the roof
of all things, where wishes
line up like children
waiting for their wings to dry,
planning to leap, catch air, fly off.

This ladder's slick glass ribs
won't hold toes or fingernails.
Tiny climbers slide from its tip
all afternoon, become a puddle
then ice again by dusk.

You may embrace this icicle
at its thickest place, big as the thigh
of a frozen man, its tip delicate
as a nipple, the whole thing hanging
twelve feet long.

Light passes through, and shadow,
but the house across the street,
seen through its distortion
looks like a blurt of ink
splattered on clean snow.

Perhaps it will fall before it melts
or melt before it falls,
its molecules reassembling
underground, filtering forever away
from the shape it was,

a one-time deal, a collaboration
of water and chill and gravity,
a directional sign for all life,
an image of accumulation,
a good use of negative space.

Girl in the Doorway, January Dawn

From where I sit
in the frozen air of my car, waiting
for engine parts to warm,
she looks like a small ghost
floating in yellow light from the hall.
Her hand is pressed
against the glass, the blue astronauts
of morning scattering in the sky
across her shirt.

Slowly, the dull cold and dark
is peeling back, exposing again
a city beneath, almost beautiful,
its light rippling out across
the pale brown linen of hills
flanking the shallow Platte, ice-fringed
and sluggish at it drains northeast.

Eventually, she will go from me
and from my house,
the door then closed to my leaving,
no smudged handprint left behind.
I want to remember her disheveled hair
and the way she stands, not yet level
with the door's brass handle
having risen for just this,
to see her father off to work.

Poem for a Cold Walk Home

If I told my story, you might doubt
how high snow piled along the street,
how smooth the ice lay all about

low places in a glassy sheet,
green and black as dusk came down,
late January freeze complete.

I measured steps, a little clown,
with songs and jokes, the squirrels and birds
the only audience around.

I think they knew the tunes and words
but were too cold to sing along;
instead the wind pulled minor chords

across the weedy fields, a throng
of silver maples, branches bare,
conducting our shared winter song

with clacking tips in swirling air.
Halfway home I left the road
for a secret path in the forest where

a frozen stream, swept clean and hard,
curved off toward my father's place
and passed the boundary of our yard.

I worked to free each frozen lace,
exchanged my boots for battered skates,
fat snowflakes falling on my face.

My mother would be setting plates
on the kitchen table, still warm
loaves of bread on cooling grates.

Then I would move with the wind, the berm
of snow on either side my shield
from the now advancing storm.

I skated curves and leapt the stones
protruding from imperfect ice
until I saw the lights of home.

Sometimes I finished with a jump, twice
as high as the banks of snow,
landing with a sweet release

deep in a drift. Sometimes I know
I stopped and stared into the rooms,
dark shapes in foursquare panes, below

the chimney's smoking plume.
So I return now, years gone by,
my memories a winter bloom.

How Spring Arrives

First, she looks at you with those green eyes
and you feel something give way inside, a barrier
so old and ready, there is no sensation
of loss. Behind her, across the field, the craggy elms
flaunt their mossy hues, the brilliant yellow-greens
mixed winter-long in dormant buds.
You see across her collarbone the skin flush red,
the rising and falling, the oxygen you share
this April afternoon, when everyone has gone
deep into ignorance, everyone but you. The point
is to not touch her. Your hands know gentleness
and yet she hasn't come for that and no caress
can ever mean as much as this, a moment pure
and slow, when nothing must be said.

When We Win the Little League Game

It's 96°, the field's as hard and dry as
sandstone in noon sun.
The parents of the other team

clean fangs with splintered bats,
deep guttural sounds spill from the shade
underneath the trees.

The umpire's a sportscaster
from Channel 9, or used to be,
before the bald spot grew too obvious.

The scorched crows in the cottonwoods
call phrases from Ty Cobb's book,
hook slide with cleats high,

until the players take the field, mostly cherubs
with small gloves, the catcher's thick glasses
glinting behind his mask.

Second base may explode, the bleachers
may combust spontaneously,
no doubt the game would still take place.

It takes the heart of a kid
to cut through all this crap.
Maybe he makes a diving stop at short

and throws the runner out
to the cheer that will not be suppressed,
so sudden and sincere a joy

it sparks the crows off perches into the sun
where they whirl up above the players
leaping on pitcher's mound.

Man With the Cowboy Coat

He shaved his head
or nearly

into a thatch,
a scratching post

for Wyoming wind.
But still, I doubted his coat,

mute black leather
hung to his shins,

wings at the shoulders
to keep off rain

while chasing dogies
up the rough edge

of a badlands trench
or among a sparse audience

of sage, lingering
to watch the credits roll.

Even if the man
in the cowboy coat will never

do any of those things,
he looks sharp buttoning up,

a retro-western grimace
on his face

and the scent of hide and dust
billowing about the office.

To a Friend, on the Death of Her Mother

You may hear her weeping,
her emptiness filling the space of a room
she hardly knows,

the corners abandoning light
in the morning. There's no way
to reach her, she's gone,

already gone. Let her go.
Even drifting together over sad oaks
and soft inclines of gold country,

she would leave you eventually,
her hand, her outstretched arm
receding until distance blurred

their shape. Already
youth untwines in you,
tangled as hair in motion

like the surface of a brook.
Turn to that world, to the place
of survivors, where I have lived

these few years, fatherless,
a ghost leaving scent
on my pillow, in my shirts.

The Woman With Very Pale Skin

At first, her hair seems too black,
as if wet with ink, as if
waving from the floor of an ocean crevasse,
her face, a blind fish the color of milk,
sheltered in the thick.

Then I see what it really is.
Her skin is pale, too pale
for health or the risks of air,
her arms like soft and visible bone
but for their fine strands of hair.

Perhaps the sun never touched
this woman's skin,
kept indoors, away from windows,
moving always in the wash
of fluorescent lights,

her long sleeves pulled down
to the wrist, gloves upon her hands.
Above her collarbone, a blue vein
throbs along her throat,
proof there is color within.

I know she is not well.
Later, when months have passed,
she will tell me she has leukemia,
and within days will disappear,
her stories never retrieved

from the file in my desk.
It's then I'll wonder if I should have said
how beautiful I found her pale skin,
how I wished to touch it,
how it frightened me.

Now her deep, slow voice turns
vanilla smoke in the cold afternoon,
in the space between us, and I hope
to myself there is someone
to enfold her without fear.

Kelsey on the Swing

I think you may abandon
gravity this time, swinging out over
the plush green, your tough hands

gripping the chains, your toes
pointed as I showed you once,
summers ago, myself as innocent

a father as you are a girl.
What keeps you here with me
I know: not gravity or boundary,

nothing but your youth,
which is mortal as mine was.
Still I will sit here in the shade,

watch you arc toward an apex
fore and aft, your pale hair the flag
of a nation I once lived in

and was forced to leave.
Girl with a thousand dreams,
you will not have them all

but I shall not say so,
no, not I,
here in this garden of the possible.

Part III

Not Crossing the River

Advice for Visitors to Rock Springs

If you stop at the diner
on the outskirts of town,
skip the soup full of dust
from Indian graves, the rinds of bad winters

bobbing in a mean meat broth.
Avoid the acid coffee and too-sweet pie,
avoid the chili, the stew
that will plague you until Dakota.

Whatever happens, don't fight with locals,
even over an insult. They've nothing to lose
except more years in Rock Springs,
a thousand more meals at the diner.

Ignore the buffoon at the counter
who disapproves of your skin.
His penis, sadly, was stolen by Coyote
and will never be returned.

He's searched the red desert each day since
and found the tracks circle back
to this town where, despite its name,
nothing springs form rock and rain is rare.

Leave the biggest tip you can.
Their lives will be hard and strangers
will always appear, distressed by the food
and scenery, anxious and able to leave.

Their lives will be long in dry air, hot sun,
and cold that puckers the bone.
Some day the last person left will admit
the whole place was a mistake

and closing a door, will depart,
leaving gas station signs to swing and rust,
and rabbits to inhabit the rooms
where sad-faced whores turned tricks

for truckers and dreamed of Vegas,
of one-armed bandits that came in coins
and streets lit by more than stars' dim light
and highways that led somewhere.

Four Poems From Thin Air

1. Mud Season, Flat Tops Wilderness

In good boots, each step is a comfort—
the soft squish and slide, the quick
suck of the heel extracted.

Rain this time of year
falls in a mist,
none of the malevolence

of summer's sudden thunderstorm
that rattles rocks in their sockets, stabs
hot blades into the quaking trees.

It's May, still cool this high.
I watch the crooked path
turn to a brook as afternoon comes on

and the sun gains the slope,
the meadow's hip-deep snow
from this distance a frayed quilt

stitched by wapiti tracks,
draped over deadfall and dusting
the spires of fractured trunks.

2. Never Summer

Afternoon sun already gone behind
the rim of cliffs leaves the water black.

May wind swirls, rushing among pines,
then drags a thousand fingers

across the lake, lifting lily pads
that sail where they rest,

tethered to the sandy bed below,
thatched with soft timbers.

Silver fish hover in green water
amid the odd geometry of fallen trunks.

Here, in their home, I'm ashamed
of my poor human form, floundering

in the icy water of late morning.
Birds soar up invisible spirals

reminding me I can't fly, the words
harsh in their throats.

3. Avalanches

It's hard to say whether loose rock
or soggy snow, sun-warmed,
starts the slides,

but each time it begins with a clatter
two thousand feet above spongy
alpine tundra. Chutes, couloirs

disgorge dark soil like
muddied river rapids
in vertical flow.

The spillage roars, dividing itself
on boulders and outcrops, finishing
at the basin in folds and ripples,

the arrested motion of a waterfall
frozen, then half-melted,
discolored as oatmeal, rocks for raisins.

Avalanches fall all afternoon today,
even a late one, after hours of stillness,
bursts from the gate at the mountain top,

scree and talus tumbling
along with the backpacks of climbers
shivering in side crevices

as snow rushes past, flushing out
the gap, its slow and punishing
delivery complete at last.

Solstice, the longest hours of June sun,
still can't slip the hinge of cornices
etching shadows on the glare

of immaculate white slopes.
Chiaroscuro, bas-relief,
water sculpted by cold and wind

from the peak. These avalanches
emanate from a single
crack in the striated surface.

From below they grow
wider and spend themselves,
tongues hanging out of a mouth.

4. Where the Forest Grows Still

Late afternoon, the sun moves behind
a high ridge and snow,
sun-warmed only moments ago,
turns from softness to crust. I slow, then stop,
my skis no longer slicing, and sounds
emerge: wind rushing down valley,
setting the limbs of the firs to trembling.

Here at 8,000 feet, on this trail
between two old mining towns,
I am finally not alone.

Man Approaching on Bourbon Street

There is a man coming the other way
on Bourbon Street. He's ragged, he parts

the revelers as a stone
parts the river, his clothes

damp with urine, his eyes
black holes in a sallow face.

He lurches forward, barely erect,
as drinkers skim by,

sipping green or pink daiquiris, the man
a mere hallucination interrupting swallows.

How hollow his cheeks are—what happened
to this man? He's a husk

wrung dry of whiskey, his lips
hang loose, their trembling

the vestige of some miserable speech.
In the loud and gaudy night, an envelope

of silence surrounds him, he parts the blare
of horns that pours from nightclub doors

as a stone parts the water. Concrete has
infused his face, cruel sidewalk pillows

and newspaper sheets
abrading and staining his skin.

Perhaps some voodoo shop will steal
what's left of him when he falls,

pestle his bones to powder,
a charm against cirrhosis,

or distill what fluids remain into
a potion to bring on delirium.

In the hot, moist air of this place
his desiccated frame draws off the excess

pleasure and feigned joy of liquors,
the swollen fun of tourists,

the cool electric spark in the blood.
This ghost of Mardi Gras Past is real,

moving against the flow of foot traffic,
on this street but not of this dimension,

a blue clown without greasepaint,
dragging an invisible corpse behind him.

In Her Black Hair

When you swim there
with your eyes,
long strands pull like kelp,

soft across your calluses.
It's not beauty,
that old caress, that draws you down

but the taste of mint and salt
at the back of your throat,
same taste

upon her tongue you know
as well as language
that fills space

between the vibrant atoms
of her few words.
You cannot disappear

in her black hair.
See in the glass
her shoulder exposed

as fronds part in September wind.
Even innocent fascination
with this wet garden

of thoughts
sets you moving through the growth
where you always break off limbs,

sure you once knew
not to drown, knew
the way back through her hair.

So you don't dive, you turn
from that black splash, thighs parting
glossy water, moving you to shore.

Third Base

That day he saw the sky go black
behind the backstop, wet air rising
and turning counterclockwise,
all the people on the bleachers oblivious
as the leaves contorted and grew pale
and silence was broomed before the storm
until it overtook the field,
and he wondered if the bases
were strapped down, imagined them
sucked up with him into the funnel
where terrific winds would spin him
together with car tires, Ted's dog, small trees,
the whole thing jolting as it skipped
across town, pulverizing
houses and stores with its tip,
and as he imagined all this,
Tommy Corcoran smacked a one-hopper
his way at third base,
striking him on the chin.

Why I'm Bleeding

The jagged metal sliced through seven layers of skin,
exposing the workings of knuckle, pale blue cartilage
and sinews grey, the mechanisms of gripping and turning,
the means by which anything is ever in hand.

The doctor rinsed the stiff blood from the wound
so it bled fresh, a red so bright against the gauze
and the porcelain sink it pulled every red with it
down the drain, leaving the air still and bleached.

Then the sutures: one, two, three, four,
the needle like a de-barbed hook pierced
flesh on either side of the gash; then the thread
tightening, the neat loop and knot, the closing again.

There's a thrill, a scary beauty, in a deep, clean cut.
Suddenly, your body is yours again, it belongs
wholly to you and throb throb—you remember
you're a soft thing moving in a world of edges.

We're made to bleed. It's easy to forget, to lose
all sense of the river that runs through us all,
until, surprise, an accident releases that
brilliant color, the warm copper and salt, the self.

Why the Lonely Cowboy Kicked a Hole in the Bathroom Wall of Room 235 at the Budget Inn, Evanston, Wyoming

bad TV reception

waitress in Elko didn't get his joke about the two cops
    and the hooker

looked in the mirror at his tattoo

road food gave him diarrhea

still 100 miles or so from Rock Springs

pointed boots make neat, round holes in plaster walls

had that nightmare again the last three nights and he
    can't stay awake much longer

she won't marry him, not now, not ever

worried about the sore on his gums, right where he
    tucks his chew

Lost $350 and a night's sleep playing $5 slots in Reno

turned 34 this year

some nights, when it gets real quiet, like it is tonight

Black Ice

On the longest night she cannot see
that winter will ever pass.
She cannot wait for the instant when
solstice folds like an envelope
around itself and slips
the other way, the nights
then growing shorter.
She takes a handgun you once held,
leaves the bedroom door
ajar, leaves her child, her child's father,
in the presence of ghosts
whose frozen feet polish the streets
when the moon grows pale, leaves town.
Outside, black ice reflects
the red tongue stoplight flicking,
flicking in a predawn dream
as she enters the room,
takes the shirt from her shoulders, hangs it
over the mirror, reads
the last chapter of a novel she loves,
holds the bullets
in the pink flesh of her hand, they are
little leaden headaches, heavy tears
so hard to shed.

Not Crossing the River

We are sitting at the edge of the prairie,
                      together but not touching.

Now it's a parking lot, a hot day, the asphalt
            in the distance writhing under waves of heat.

A bird flies overhead, circles higher, and again.

We are watching two boys eat ice cream as they
                  lean against the storefront.

Now we are driving a gauntlet of blue sage, tough,
               low-growing, buffeted by wind.

You have fallen asleep in the front seat.

It begins to rain lightly and the windshield wiper
                on my side leaves a smear.

I know that for breakfast, you will order eggs,
                toast, grapefruit juice.

We are in a restaurant in a small town in Indiana,
        just after dawn, already hot, and you drink your juice.

The convenience store clerk is crying softly
              when I come in to pay for gas.

Now we walk along a ruined beach and your foot snags
           on old fishing line discarded among the rocks.

For a short stretch, there is roadkill every 50 yards
                along the shoulder.

Traffic slows, people looking out their windows
           at the man being fitted with a neck brace.

The hum of cicadas grows to a crescendo, then subsides.

On the map, you find a town named "Gamble,"
                                             another "Far Cry."

We sit at the edge of a river wide and muddy, and know
                                          that we won't cross.

Come Back, Brother Thomas

1

I saw you often in the cold little town,
its rigid sheet of snow
blacked with grime and shrunken

to dense berms along the streets.
Most mornings you carried books
and heavy bags, sometimes

the burdens of others, like once
when you bore an enormous
blond cross, the blood of a monk

who'd made the right choice
at the wrong time
still drying in the joints of wood.

2

The ice grows so hard and sleek the holy ghost
could skate without his blades, with just
the hard bones of his heels to slide, one foot
across and over, ever over, into turns.
If I were a man, if I were muscle, bone,
and skin, he'd say to no one there, I'd
cross this frozen lake though it be
many miles broad and winds
would tear my robe to shreds.

Instead, it's just a frigid Saturday
in a cold little town and one man skates
among a group of boys and girls,
some clinging to his sleeves, these children
on the brink of disappearing,
sure you'd come from behind the statue
of Francis, guarding his forgotten altar.

3

At night, a book opens on the desk
in your room. You sleep on.
The pages are illuminated
by light you'll never see, despite

what you've been told. Gold, red, and yellow
leaves entwine the shapes of women,
the shapes of men, a godhead above
and below, the whiptail of a beast.

Dust of desiccated skin blooms
above the page, an invisible hand
passes over text, a haunted, soundless
recitation beginning again.

4

Mornings we shoveled the light snow away,
to find night wind had polished
the ice to black glass our skates could carve
with thin script, delicate loops and whirls.
That day we thought for sure
you'd come, play shinny with us,
tell your stories while we caught our breath
and sipped hot cocoa from the thermos
one mother made us bring. Sometimes
you'd given us books, and we always hoped
for more, hoped you'd stay and translate
as no one ever had. We never thought
they'd send you so far away. We stayed
that day until the sun gave up
and darkness closed the vacant fields, stayed
until one girl's dad came slipping across
the length of ice to gently call us home.
That's when we knew, as sure as a crack
can open and a body disappear
down through forty feet of chill,
that you were gone.

5
You might have been just 25-years-old,
ancient in your youth, a slow smile
proof you'd aged beyond your years.

Who came to announce the news
that you must go? Was it the one with
the empty porcelain face, a man

who would surely understand?
Was it the crippled one, little scepter
in his hand, the recurrent boil

on his neck now purple with cold rage,
his legs moving stiffly, stabbing
the earth as he crossed?

Who came to tell you, and did he knock
or simply enter your small room,
with its bookcase, its desk and one lamp

glowing in the early morning dimness?
We heard you had to leave your books
behind, and wondered why.

6
You should know
we begged them.
They would never tell us
where you went.

Fourth Bout With Lightning Proves Fatal
for Stevensville Man

Six weeks back a bolt struck Roger's truck.
Blue sparks danced on radio keys
and back tires burned to grease,
their double-snake signature shed

on southbound Highway 93.
What luck, the policeman joked,
stroking the vinyl of the truck's
bowed dash, brushing strands of

singed hair off Roger's coat.
Struck twice as a child,
that was his third shock
but it was not to be his last.

Yesterday, on Georgetown Lake,
as he piloted his aluminum craft
a mile from shore, a tarp for a coat,
a half-foot of water in the ribs of the boat,

Roger never heard the crack
of the bolt. Maybe it just
scared him to death, one friend proposed.
His fishing buddies felt a faint pulse

but couldn't heave his 300 pounds
from boat to dock. They left him
slumped against the oars and gunwale,
a creel for a pillow.

The sheriff, kneeling in the rain,
pronounced him dead.
Roger had swept the high school halls
each night for twenty-seven years,

humming beneath fluorescent lights.
The night the bolt blew his car radio,
he must have felt the tires melt, as hailstones
pinged off the pickup's roof.

Out on the lake he must have known
to flee black clouds gathering over
the Sapphire Range, and flee he did,
the outboard motor whining in the rain.

He fled too late. Maybe in the flash he saw
again that instant when he stood
in puddled mud, just 10-years-old,
the hair upon his arms and neck

rising, falling, a field of grass in wind,
and there he was, a small electric thing
about to glow like Franklin's key
at the kite-string's end.

We'll Drive to Nebraska

Even when the wind stops, the oaks
keep swaying and what little rain
makes it to the earth can't darken dirt
or quench the great thirst of tallgrass prairie.
Let's say your dog died weeks ago
and it rained hard that day, stubborn spring
refusing to let mud dry, refusing even
sensible requests for warmth.
Let's say he died and you wept,
though not as I thought you would,
your face a prairie and your tears
virga. There are a thousand lousy dying dogs
lying hunched and betrayed in cages
in every city. I saw you walk such a
gauntlet of curs, finally empty of hope
at 10 years old. But hope comes back,
even when it shouldn't. Maybe it wakes
in sunlight polishing folds and seams
of bottomland threaded with cottonwoods.
Maybe it takes a cobblestone street
in a small town, alive with barefoot kids
and a goat tethered to a front porch rail
to make you smile again, that and a litter
of 12 pups, black and tan, sable and black,
two fat as piglets, two of them mean,
one hiding behind an old crate,
eyeing you, sniffing the air and finally
stepping slowly into the light.

Redwood Villanelle

We walk a brown path cut by rivulets,
the sea air heavy, the winter light diffuse
through groves of trees as straight as minarets.

We've come far from the world of threats
and pain, from all things put to their misuse.
We walk a brown path cut by rivulets,

as friends and lovers, having no regrets,
and where it branches, we have but to choose
which grove of trees as straight as minarets.

Things are out of scale; a pale sun sets.
The winter air is cool, the light diffuse.
We walk a brown path cut by rivulets,

we turn this way or that without regrets.
May we always put our time to such good use
as here among trees straight as minarets.

There's nothing we can do to shape events;
the joys in having what you have to lose.
So walk with me through muddy rivulets,
past giant trees as straight as minarets.

High Desert Song North of Albuquerque

The brilliant sun on winter chases ice
down into red soil and everywhere shuddering stalks

survive on that water and a cold fragrant wind
heavy with knowledge of how to work stone.

You have broken your knuckles on the engine again,
blood on the greasy rag, torn skin,

but the numbness helps. That bird above
may pluck you from all this, from pale monks

inscribing the dust, from friends
whose peaceful homes lie distant

on days as short as this. A sharp moon tightens
the low edge of the sky to its mooring

on a black ridge, volcanic, pocked,
its flow arrested before an audience

of grass and cactus. In the canyons
beyond the ridge, ancients hammered

the patina, their petroglyphs a language
your congressman will never learn.

Now the sky grows orange as you watch
and flushes pink against cold air

pressing from the south. This is where
you have always lived, no matter what they say.

Ten Poems for the Growing Season

1. *Fresh Strawberries*

Heat rises from wet earth, early June morning
of a day that will blister and bake. Summer

is here, spring's cool shade and rain banished
to the high meadows. You have these rare days

alone, the quiet grass soft underfoot while overhead
a bird mother squawks at a raider jay, dives

in fury at the cat with a nestling
limp in it grinning mouth.

The sun, already hot, cannot penetrate the canopy
of deep green leaves in the strawberry patch.

Underneath, clusters of red fruit hang on tendrils
just above the soil, unblemished, perfect in their

multitude of shapes—some conical, some knotted
like small angry fists, some bulbous, and then

the sweetest ones of all, small and dark with sugar.
Pull them gently; the stems will fall away.

Rinse them with cold water from the hose.
There in your palm a breakfast best crushed

one at a time on the tongue.

2. Just After the Rainstorm

I hear water tick its way
down the leaves of the elms,
then thunder rolls miles away

as sirens race toward some disaster,
a fallen tree or man struck
by a lightning bolt.

The heat that hung like
canvas over this town is gone,
replaced by a rising musk

of wet earth. My garden
looks reborn, tassles of corn
just emerging, pale and soft,

are drenched. I pluck a tomato,
brilliant red, warm and dripping rain;
the juice bursts in my mouth.

3. Rismal

On nights when summer softness comes in dreams,
when winter's cold cuts starlight into threads
that fall upon the ice of frozen streams,

grown still around the stones set in their beds,
on nights like that I lie upon the grass
gone brown, amid old flowers with bowed heads.

Once still, I think I feel the season pass,
I feel my body's heat begin the thaw,
the earth beneath my palms a looking glass

that shows Orion's hand begin to draw
his bowstring taut, the arrow of the spring
ready to fly, to bring the natural law

that wakens roots in soil so they sing
a song of green for those now listening.

4. Poem for a September Morning

Cool, refreshing night faded so slowly from the sky
this morning, no one heard it leave. The cat woke

and stretched at the foot of the bed, then lay
her front paws on my feet, a sure sign her old

arthritic bones were seeking heat, the first time
since last April when frost coated upturned soil.

At dawn, the light was deep yellow, striking the tops
of brown-tassled corn, spreading downward over squash

and tomatoes, firing the bright red peppers, dressing
the folds of the marigolds, rejuvenating the vine.

There is never time to waste, and as you stand
in a later summer garden, color and taste filling your senses,

time slows its terrible rush, grows still as
tricks of light spark in the shade and silence.

5. Wind Rustles Corn

Wind rustles corn,
chases summer heat down alleys
toward the far edge of distant spring.
Dawn light comes late today,
sleepers in a warm embrace
ignore the pale caress
on wrist or face, burrowing
back into dreams of hot sun
that combed locks of silk,
fell on waxy leaves
of bird peppers, pooled
in the foliage of summer squash.
Sluggish bees bob and dip
over ruined blossoms.
Morning glories will last until
late afternoon, when sun slips
from behind thick clouds
to wilt a hundred blue trumpets.
First frost flows
from high peaks, a night-pulsing
glacier, a hand to close the eyes of
flowers, to cure the final fruits.
Wind rustles corn again,
the soft laughter of autumn's approach.

6. Gathering the Herbs

The papers pile high on my desk, cold fog
hovering in the late September sky as sun
makes its feeble rising. My attention wanes
from the task; such cool air I must not waste.
Outside, my shoes brush through
just-brown grass, gathering moisture. The last
strawberries hide beneath the reddening leaves,
fruit parched by near frost two nights past.
I know it's time to clip what herbs I can
before the real cold comes. I kneel
in the stone circle and take the slender stalks
of French tarragon in my hands, a pepper scent
mixing with rich tones of grass. The lemon balm
is sharp and strong, oregano and sage
blending earth and ocean spray. Sweet marjoram,
at first a subtle tang, bursts when I pull the stalks
and cut, then bind with string. Inside again,
I hang them in the cool dark basement room,
a symphony of incense for the long winter,
where all things grow quiet under snow.

7. October Sun on the Marigolds

You may say this is trivial, a fool's pursuit,
but to my eyes, the sun this morning warmed
frost away from the orange, yellow blooms
so slowly they almost came back to life.

But to my eyes, the sun this morning warmed
the soil summer parched, the heat like a mouth
so slow it almost came back to life,
yet sleep will advance again this night, again.

The soil summer parched, the heat like a mouth,
maybe the last breath of an ancient woman,
yet sleep will advance again this night, again
the rough wash of dark across the moon.

Maybe the last breath of an ancient woman
gives us all who survive in our glorious summer
the crisp edge of white around the moon,
a night of sleep outside in brilliant air.

You may say this is trivial, a fool's pursuit.
Give us another glorious summer
so slow it brings us back to life
on this, the best morning of the year.

8. *Harvest Triolet*

Sunlight strikes the vine's tendrils, threads each stalk
of corn gone brown and raspy in slight breeze.
Before the work begins, I take a walk

down rows of plants I know will freeze
this night, the last fruits finally stripped.
My labor is a prayer I'll offer on my knees.

Yesterday the marjoram was tipped
with curled black leaves, a hint of frost
to come. The roses have been clipped;

basil, thyme, tarragon I cut and bundle first,
to dry and concentrate in cool and dark,
awaiting February, when summer flavors burst

upon the tongue. This is good work,
lifting fattened pumpkins to the shelves
and turning over compost with the fork.

Cailleach, suspended from the eaves,
we'll greet your maiden daughter in the spring,
in her garments green and made of leaves.

9. Song for the Stone Girl

Ash leaves lit with sun whose arc is low;
season hurries toward where seasons go.

Stone girl, does your smile reveal the truth—
sculptor carved your face out of my youth.

Wicker basket dangling from your wrist
cannot ever hold the blooms you missed.

Gown so soft an autumn shower grieves,
dangles down to red and russet leaves.

Frost has stripped the garden of green hue;
ever do I see myself in you.

Ever will another summer rise,
warming winter's darkness from your eyes.

Years among the raspberries and birds
never once have brought from you the words,

incantations that might free your form.
Now I join you, neither of us warm.

10. The Magpie's Secret

Look, the snow can't stay
forever, spread thin as milk glass
over garden beds. Each day

it melts back, then clouds pass,
replenish its edge, then sun burns back,
marks time on bent brown grass.

Night frost glazes the spare track
a fox leaves on the field;
he survives on mice and luck.

In a dream, magpies converse
with jays beneath a low blue sky;
they quiet as you pass.

Winter ice is just a lie
in the throat, the sharp moon
never looked so high.

If you grow still you'll hear the tone
of the soil as it thaws.
Go into winter and search its rooms.

Driving Nails by Hand

I've seen every muscle she has
in flexion and repose
these fifteen years gone past,

those I first admired from afar,
the lean, taut fibers of her legs,
twin dreams of a starved boy,

and later, the smoothness of her belly,
the bending slope of a wave
past cresting.

Now, in a dusty garage we bend together
to the task of building shelves,
early June heat squeezing water

to the surface of our skin.
The power tools we borrowed
now lie still, their cruel bits

protrude silently, their wicked
scimitars the poised teeth
of a wolf turned steel

at the moment of attack.
She's driving nails by hand, hammer
to head, to head, to head

until the thin shaft sinks and disappears
in the soft slat,
faint scent of split pine emanating.

I see her perfect bicep, mounded
but not bulky, and in extension
fluid, lithe between her dimpled shoulder

and the hard bones of elbow.
The pounding of the hammer
shows everything in unison,

this woman, such a fine machine
and powerful, and graceful,
my own hand resisting the pull

of muscle and sinew that answers
some urge to reach, take gentle hold
of her arm, to feel what flows beneath.

She's driving nails by hand,
and I'm in love again today, as yesterday.
Who was I to inherit

another man's daughter
bringing children to her
through secret muscles and rivers

of my own, left now to build
and rebuild shelters for the making
of new lives?

I will take her fine bones in my own
again tonight, encircling again
the half of self that is not self

but that a man, if he is wise and
marked with luck, may find,
knowing she will answer

with her own strong embrace,
and in that temporary union
we will build a lasting house.

In the Forest of Ruined Trees

I hold your hand in this strange glen,
the skinny pines now turned to rust
so dry the needles arch for rain.
I hold your hand in this strange glen,
and wonder how, and wonder when.
We walk bare floors, sift lunar dust,
I hold your hand in this strange glen,
the skinny pines now turned to rust.

The mine above, its yellow beard
of arsenic pouring toward the creek,
a thing the dead have never feared.
The mine above, its yellow beard,
a hundred years, a hundred years
the gaping mouth has meant to speak.
The mine above, its yellow beard
of arsenic pouring toward the creek.

We rise above the blue grey town
as clouds stack on the granite crest.
The ghosts of birds fly upside down,
high above the blue grey town,
its orange lake of sludge a crown,
we see from where we take our rest.
We turn back toward the blue grey town
as clouds stack on the granite crest.

Dry lightning flashes from the skies,
the finger of a healing flame.
I hold your hand and close my eyes;
dry lightning flashes from the skies,
I see the blaze ignite and rise,
the light inside me as I dream.
Dry lightning flashes from the skies
the finger of a healing flame.

Leaving Iowa City, Late Summer

All night while we slept, the rolling hills
murmured in their green cloaks and shook
the tasseled corn till clouds of pale yellow dust
rose up into the sky. At dawn, cool mists
hung over the highway, and passing through them
I grew full of a strange longing to stay.
I could live on the river, listening
to the slap and gurgle of lazy water,
watching the hawks circle and dive.
I could grow used to the song of the locusts,
abrading moist darkness at midnight.
I could blend into the foot traffic
by the cafe downtown, lost for a time
on unfamiliar streets, living by the generosity
of strangers. I thought these things as morning came,
summer fog flowing down the contours of farms,
the air warming under gentle sun as we drove west.

Drinking Beer With Lincoln

You're surprised to find him there
in the spot where Booth shot him,
where he originally slumped over,

his wife frozen, unable to speak,
99 years before Jackie
climbed over the trunk.

He agrees to join you next door
for a drink, so you walk together
down the narrow theater stairs.

His face is haggard as in the last photos,
but animated, it grows handsome,
this no plaster likeness lifted

as the last breath cleared his frame.
At the bar, Lincoln drinks slowly, talks of
his terrible dream, the sound of weeping

he followed through the halls. Not heard again
till Nixon, he says, laughing just a little.
I was hated more

in my four years of war, he says.
You should have seen the bodies
piled on the banks at Fredericksburg,

that idiot Burnside
sending waves of men against the city
until twelve thousand died.

Grant perfected it, called it
war of attrition.
He finishes his beer and stands to leave.

His fingers float through
overcoat sleeves, then he grasps
your hand and pumps it twice

as a president would. You're surprised
how cool his flesh, and how airy.
Strange that no one notices

it's Lincoln striding between the tables,
excusing himself and deferring to ladies,
stovepipe hat in hand.

The play is about to begin
back at the theatre, and he's expected
to be there in his chair,

to take the bullet again,
to give the last full measure
of his devotion.

After a Performance of the Scottish Play

In low light, after all the patrons leave,
a stagehand mops the fake blood from the boards.
No one is left to hear the lady grieve
in low light, after all the patrons leave.
She's backstage, rinsing fake blood from her sleeve,
her head still humming from remembered words.
In low light, after all the patrons leave,
a stagehand mops the fake blood from the boards.

In the parking lot, the actor waits,
imagining the three Weird Sisters come,
imagining them as the mythic fates,
in the parking lot, the actor waits,
aware the play is done, aware he hates
the moment of his cue: "A drum, a drum . . ."
In the parking lot, the actor waits,
imagining the three Weird Sisters come.

Backstage, the sabers tremble in their sheaths,
the cauldron once again begins to steam.
The pilot's thumb grows warm, a costume breathes,
backstage, the sabers rattle in their sheaths.
The stagehand locks the door before he leaves,
sure what he heard and saw was but a dream
when backstage, sabers rattled in their sheaths
and the cauldron once again began to steam.

How a Fox Disappears

A rustle in the willows as day turns dark;
she's almost invisible, covering ground
in failing light, her coat of rust and black
threads through the willows as day turns dark,
in soft river mud she leaves her track.
Then beyond the bend you hear the sound;
a rustle in the willows as day turns dark;
she's almost invisible, covering ground.

Grey trunks of cottonwoods lean into winter,
the river grown sluggish, shallow and still,
islands and shoals formed in the center
where grey trunks of cottonwoods lean into winter.
She moves through the willows, necessity sent her
to fill up the hunger she never can fill.
Grey trunks of cottonwoods lean into winter,
the river grown sluggish, shallow and still.

Then she emerges from cover and runs,
loping across the wide field of bent grass,
her agile black paws clatter on stones.
She darts from the bank to the cover and runs,
as night overwhelms and softens the tones
from gold to dun and you see her at last—
she breaks from the riverbend willows and runs,
loping across a wide field of bent grass.

Gathering Chokeberries Along
the River Bottom, Late August

The air is spiced with scents of rotting wood,
long grass, and musky underbrush, the sun
illuminating soil where spring flood
left tangles of bare branches on its run
down to the plains. This summer's rains
left all things green this late, and as I step
between the fallen trunks I see the chains
of red-black cherries dangling, heavy, ripe.
A sudden blur of motion, cracking brush,
a buck then flashes from a hidden place
and seizes up just yards away, the hush
around us loud as we stand face to face.
I leave the lowest cherries, reach instead
for branches thick with fruit above my head.

How We Could Spend the Winter Together

We could lie down in the garden, beneath
the first snow, lie among broken
stalks of corn, near the row of tired onions

and the few last bean pods, long and brown,
withered as a saint's relic hung
on a trellis near the Himalayan vine.

Would you lie beside me?
The cold snap of flakes upon our faces
might teach us to hold sensations

so they resonate and melt away.
We'd talk about another winter night,
twenty years ago, and time

would melt away. If your hand were in mine,
we could talk by touch
as January turned dry, grass bent

toward February, drifting with its prow
the color of a thaw, its mast scrolling
from star to star on a black page above.

Imagine how it would feel—the sun
on us both that first hot day. We'd wake
from whatever slumber we'd found,

stand and shake our limbs, comb
the leaves from each other's hair.
A kiss or an embrace would be fine.

There's more time left for us, here
in the midst of our garden,
as the shortest day of winter

billows down the canyons west
and leaves the driest snow on earth,
a foot deep, a bed for winter sleep.

Fin Dome

For Art Skaife

1

Among the few trees that grow high,
that survive and survive, that live
despite incessant wind and the brief

Sierra summer above 10,000 feet,
there is a pine whose bark, crossed
with rich, dark crevasses,

leaks vanilla, thick and soft, almost
liquid. But to know this one must
bend to tree, bury the nose

in the rough surface, lose
all other senses: the sound of picas
chippering from rocky outcrops,

the sight of ouzels diving upstream
like grey-feathered salmon, a breeze cooling
the thin film of sweat

along the small of your back. One must lose
all this and remember only
to breathe.

2

At some elevations, the lakes at noon will undulate
from lapis to azure, green bottoms so dark
only pure black is missing. As midday heat
retreats, before the longest shadows crawl
the surface swallowing every hue, cutthroat
rise, the bowtips of an underwater
orchestra, leaping, random, leaving only
spreading circles to ripple down to glass again.
After the fish have fed, then is the time
to swim, to enter the water naked
and unsure, the water so cold it seems
on loan from an old blue glacier.

3

One sometimes finds
blackened rocks
used to hem a fire
lit by one who tore
gnarled branches
from a low, earth-hugging
dwarf pine
demarcating treeline,
tree but two feet high
and three centuries old.

4

It is best to leave the peaks by noon,
before sparks gather on the tongues of clouds,

before snow grows dense in sun and sags,
breaks loose, brings chunks of rock and mud

down couloirs in a liquid rush that sweeps men
before it or buries them head down, helpless.

It is best to leave no signs, or else just footprints
in the wet mud rim around receding lakes. It is best

to slow traverse the steep-sloped field of ice,
pocked with bowls where water gathers in the sun.

If you slip, roll and bury
the head of the ax deep.

5

I will take your hand, grandfather,
firmly in my own, your skin thin and soft,
as an insect's wing. We'll walk to Fin Dome
over talus and scree, beneath

a fierce blue sky. Forget
that your legs are weak, forget
how often you stop to rest and breathe.
The path was never less steep,

but we will not speak of this.
Some day, I'll be the old man in the house,
all my mountains memories, my
shoulders hanging inward, the points

of faint stars, the frame of an ancient tree,
a pyre before it burns. Don't be ashamed.
Sequoias take their time but in turn fall
and return to soil, still majestic on the

forest floor, a home for smaller creatures.
I found you lying on your bed, struggling
to breathe in sleep, and turned away.
I must not be ashamed; like a shaman

I must enter your dream and find you,
hiding like a child in a dark cave.
Then you will always be the young man
in the photograph, boots caked

with mud, one propped on a boulder,
near a twisted piñon stubbornly growing
in a field of exfoliated stone.
Come, we'll go again to Fin Dome,

where your feet will carry you over
the gravelly ground, through
dense stands of aromatic willow
and soft across the spongy alpine turf.

Femme Osage

Between limestone bluffs and the low, distant bank
the slow brown Missouri pushed toward ocean,
the floodplain steaming in July heat, black earth
bristling with corn, shrill insect songs

teeming in the throats of tributaries
choked with silt, with trunks and branches
of great trees, with green and tangled growth
encroaching every fecund inch that wasn't tilled.

We stopped along a dirt road, seeking shade
and a place to eat a poor lunch—crackers, plums
water gone warm in the plastic jug, the last handful
of dried apples from beautiful Maryland hills.

Sometimes, it's the wrong turn you make in places
like this, the accidental left, nudged by spirits
who recognize you, know your face when it belonged
to a sad soldier in butternut grey, to a tired woman

washing shirts on the rocks, to a child running
along the still stream under a canopy of green.
So we knew that we were lost, saw the road narrow
and rise, then weave the boundaries of small farms

where no one moved in the torrid noon. Then,
a crossroads. We turned left again, hoping
for highway, and the road dipped into Femme Osage,
its low brick school gone liquid with heat

and the steeple, thin and white, just piercing
a thick grove of oaks. Again, the incessant hum
of insects turned the air electric and it grew loud
amid the gravestones, leaning and fallen in a yard

just 50 feet square. No gate prevented access, no sign
marked the perimeter, the tablets marched right up
to the windows of the church, the lawn pocked
with low depressions where the residents returned

to earth, the only cool ones on this day. My daughter,
only 10, was too afraid to follow. She stood defiant
at the road, arms crossed and face set in a frown,
as if we dishonored the lonely dead to walk among

the stones. There were few names to read; rain
and sun, heat and chill, had smoothed the letters
and dates, carved in German script: *geb und gest*,
born and died, dates too close on most of them.

I ran my fingers over one small stone, deciphering
Anna Alwina Lissette Knippenberg,
geb 22 September 1863,
gest 21 July 1864. What killed you, little girl?

And then beside her stone, three more. A brother
not much older, dead on the same day.
Father and mother, forever embracing death, dead
just one day later. Was it pestilence or civil war,

some violent end or slow fever, diphtheria
creeping upriver and along the verdant glens,
taking whole families like this? My children
whirled at cemetery's edge, laughter trickling

through burned grass, stirring heavy air.
I felt my woman's hand take mine, her skin moist
and the gentle pressure on my palm familiar.
So we moved away, across the graves once more

and looking back I saw again the little plot where no one
was remembered, soft limestone sloughing names and dates,
dissolving epitaphs, cut there on summer mornings
when sorrows found families like sheaves.

The Man Who Stopped Talking
to His Wife

1

He held her before dawn,
the quiet sifting down upon them
like ancient dust.

2

She held their daughter, her cries
subsiding, small body trembling
from exertion, fury spent.

He turned from them, looked out
on tall grass, bowed
by frozen rain.

3

They walked across the lot,
black ice slick, and she slipped,
reached out to gain her balance:

her grip
on his arm.

4

He found her comb,
black against the sink's porcelain rim.
Long auburn strands.

5

They sat across from each other,
the table between them
an ocean, or a path.

She examined her hands, skin
tough with weather and use.
He took those hands in his.

6

His breathing slowed, his face
tight in concentration.
She was the only one there to see.

If You Can Hear the Song of This River

The smooth stones lie draped with green lace,
dry, tangled sticks, bones of fish, stinky mud.

Aromas rise and blend in September sun
as a Great Blue Heron glides into the willows.

The river is low, dun-colored, quietly
slipping toward Nebraska with its cargo of silt,

the last trickles of snowmelt from high cirques
and the spare rain of a stingy summer

its only sustenance. You unwrap your lunch:
red apple crisps and tart that paints your chin,

a wedge of mellow cheese and broken crackers,
a bottle of blackberry mead—homage to drowsy bees

now falling from circling routes into the murk.
You'll never come again into this noon,

to the bank of this particular river to share
with the heron the silent watch beneath the peaks

dusted white against brilliant blue. It's true,
the river will remain, another noon and another.

Another heron will land midstream on the boulder,
to wait for other trout to flutter through shallows.

But you are like the water, moving through the scene
and beyond, bent by banks, stirred by snags, pulled

through narrows and parted by rocks. Your landscape
lies ahead and the autumn shade you occupy

is an eddy, a temporary song of color and scent,
a brief rest before you run again.

Three Pecos Poems

For Tom

1. Bluebird Ranch, Villanueva

This is what happens to metal, proud shine
painted with rain for years
now sealed in cinnamon patina.
Trucks, tractors, spindly combines
melt into the weeds,
the spade-shaped leaves of wild squash
writhing along curves like a lover's arms.
Weathered wood door
of the farmhand's shed
won't budge. Behind the window,
a white enamel sink
shines. The abandoned bed, its sheets
rumpled from one last sleep, leans
into the wall beneath a tin placard
tilting from its last nail—innocent girl,
cheeks still rosy, forever spilling oranges
from a basket at her hip. Every step
falls between rust and rotted wood. Disk blades
that never will bite black earth again
lie stacked like dirty plates. A bin of bolts
and square nuts pours its oxidized
waterfall of angles. Thick chains hang,
lazy tongues waiting until words come back.
Spiders have draped their threads across
steering wheels of ghost trucks,
sunk to their bellies in dust, cracked windows
echoing the webs. Incessant wind
long since wrestled everything down
and now is left to caress still shapes
and whistle through hollow tools.

Decay comes after peace, after
striving stops, after the last slick palm
puts the pickaxe down, to lean forever
against the freewheel, finally slowed.

2. *Abandoned Baseball Field, San Miguel*

Beyond the left field fence
cottonwoods clap in the sudden wind.

A unflower bends
where shortstops stood

up on toes, blue lizards ready
to dart to the hole.

It's been so long
since a slugger sent the ball

deep, all cheers have been swallowed
by dust and vultures.

Now jimson weed claims
both batters' boxes,

pitcher's mound, both dugouts,
and cicada pulse in the heat.

Maybe last night's rain
threatened a ghost game,

the umpire finally raising his arms
to signal time was forever out

as thunderheads boomed,
white arrows flashed

on the outfield grass, and
mad wind erased the diamond.

3. Night to Morning on the Promontory

Last night coyotes cried
one song—but how many voices?
Six or eight, a raw chorus
of joy, or a call
to some jackrabbit's carcass,
warm blood seeping
over sandstone
on the banks of the Pecos,
sluggish with summer's red silt.

Last night one stone fell
from the belt of Perseus,
its yellow tail burst red,
then the green gas flare
hung in the black.
All night bright strings
laced the sky until low clouds
cruised across the mesa,
soaking red earth with rain,
pulling perfume from sage.

This morning swallows dart
along the promontory
stitching together the circling
shadows of vultures as they
ripple loosely over the cholla.
Two doves land in the juniper,
coo quiet songs and cattle
sing their ignorant lyrics
far below in drifting light and shade.

In the Morning Hours

In the morning hours, before the magpies start
their angry cawing from the trees, before
emergent sun, before the air is filled with soot

and car exhaust, and parched soil begs more
liquid night from a stingy, brightening sky,
in those morning hours you will close the door

of our room, gently, so there is no cry
from our daughter in her bed just down the hall,
so nothing can impede us as we try.

the now familiar fit of our smooth skin, the silent call
of mouth to mouth, the sacred and the only heat
we truly give away, moving in a pool

of pale blue light that gathers at our heads and feet.
The life so short, the craft so long to learn,
but I will hold you in the morning hours, sweet

beyond all hours of the day, though they burn
away before we master anything of touch,
even as we lose the thing for which we yearn

the most, the lingering here on a warm beach
lost in time, again until tomorrow out of reach.